Cinders

CARY WOLFE, SERIES EDITOR

Jacques Derrida
Cinders

Translated by
Ned Lukacher

Introduction by
Cary Wolfe

posthumanities 28

University of Minnesota Press
MINNEAPOLIS
LONDON

"Feu la cendre" was first published in *Anima* 5 (December 1982): 45–99. With the addition of the Prologue and some revisions, *Feu la cendre* was published simultaneously as a book and a cassette recording in 1987 in the series Bibliothèque des Voix by Éditions des femmes. *Feu la cendre* copyright 1987 Des femmes (Antoinette Fouque, 35 rue Jacob, 75006 Paris, France).

First published in English by University of Nebraska Press in 1991

First University of Minnesota Press edition, 2014

English translation copyright 1991 by University of Nebraska Press

This edition copyright 2014 by the Regents of the University of Minnesota

Published by the University of Minnesota Press
111 Third Avenue South, Suite 290
Minneapolis, MN 55401–2520
http://www.upress.umn.edu

LIBRARY OF CONGRESS CATALOGING-IN-PUBLICATION DATA
Derrida, Jacques.
[Feu la cendre. English]
Cinders / Jacques Derrida ; Translated by Ned Lukacher ; Introduction by Cary Wolfe. (Posthumanities ; 28)
Includes bibliographical references.
ISBN 978-0-8166-8953-8 (hc)—ISBN 978-0-8166-8954-5 (pb)
1. Plays on words. 2. Homonyms. 3. Ambiguity. I. Lukacher, Ned, 1950– II. Title. P304.D4713 2014
401'.41—dc23   2014007469

Printed on acid-free paper

UMP LSI

CONTENTS

INTRODUCTION

Cinders after Biopolitics

CARY WOLFE

"I shall speak of ghost *[revenant]*, of flame, and of ashes." So read the first words of Jacques Derrida's book *Of Spirit: Heidegger and the Question*, a text published in 1987, five years after the text you have before you.[1] *Of Spirit* is but one of the texts by Derrida that form a vast echo chamber for this work of the very slightest inscription, as if it were itself written in smoke. In many ways, *Cinders* (or *Feu la cendre*) is above all a book about spectrality, a theme that Derrida would develop on a much larger canvas roughly a decade later in *Specters of Marx*—a book that also begins with a haunting (namely, of Hamlet by the ghost of his murdered father).[2] Indeed, *Cinders* is haunted by the strange and nearly untranslatable phrase *il y a là cendre* that Derrida circles back to time and again in this text, tracing its first appearance in the front matter of *La Dissémination* in 1972 and its manifestations earlier and later (and in

1. Jacques Derrida, *Of Spirit: Heidegger and the Question*, trans. Geoffrey Bennington and Rachel Bowlby (Chicago: University of Chicago Press, 1989), 1. Further references are given in the text.
2. Jacques Derrida, *Specters of Marx*, trans. Peggy Kamuf (New York: Routledge, 1994).

different guises) in "Plato's Pharmacy" (1968), *Glas* (1974), *The Postcard* (1980), and other texts, the relevant passages of which appear on the left-hand pages of the text before you. These form the "Animadversions" to which the text occupying the right-hand pages responds, as it were—sometimes directly, sometimes obliquely and without comment.[3]

As if this weren't already intriguing enough, Derrida and Carole Bouquet recorded on cassette a "polylogue" for Antoinette Fouque's *Éditions des Femmes*, a weave of their voices reading the text of *Feu la cendre* to accompaniment, here and there, by Stockhausen's *Stimmung* (itself in turn a score for six voices), which was released with the 1987 French edition of this book. Architecturally speaking, this fact recursively doubles, but nonlinearly and asymmetrically, the double structure already at work in the text, and in ways that bear directly on Derrida's well-known philosophical investigations of the status of the voice and its manifold relations not just to self-presence and autoaffection generally but also to technologies of inscription, archivization, and memory. At this juncture we can already look back—or is it forward?—with renewed interest to Derrida's assertion in the very first sentence of *Of*

3. As Ned Lukacher notes in his original introduction to this translation, "Animadversions" means "observations" or "assessments" and "is of long standing in the history of criticism (Milton and Leibniz, for example, wrote texts using this title)." See Ned Lukacher, "Introduction: Mourning Becomes Telepathy," in Jacques Derrida, *Cinders*, trans. Ned Lukacher (Lincoln: University of Nebraska Press, 1991), 7.

Spirit that "I shall *speak*"—not "write"—"of ghost [*revenant*], of flame, and of ashes."

At least since the early work *Speech and Phenomena* (1967), Derrida has been widely understood (not without reason) to be a critic, even enemy, of the voice, whether in his dismantling the voice as a figure of self-presence and autoaffection in Husserl or his deconstruction of the elevation of speech over writing in Saussure. Stanley Cavell, for example, in a sustained encounter with Derrida's thought on the subject called "Counter-Philosophy and the Pawn of Voice," applauds Derrida's critique of what he calls "the voice of metaphysics, philosophy's hoard."[4] And yet, he writes of Derrida: "he makes it his business to monitor and to account for its encroachments while seeming, or giving the impression to some that he means, to be speaking in it, no one more cheerfully." What Derrida wants, Cavell argues, is the "final overcoming" of voice, a tidy disposal of the problem that will "end philosophically"—that will end, that is to say, with the same philosophical confidence with which voice is asserted as a figure of self-presence in Husserl (62). But as the "Prologue" you are about to read makes clear, what Cavell wants—call it an "ethics" of voice, one that does not use "philosophy" to flee from the voice as the site of "the ordinary" and "the everyday" (62)—is precisely what Derrida explores

4. Stanley Cavell, *A Pitch of Philosophy* (Cambridge: Harvard University Press, 1994), 62. Further references are given in the text.

in the opening pages of *Cinders*. Here, we find not one voice but many—and whose?—including (and not least) the "fatally silent call" of the phrase *il y a là cendre* around which the text is built; the "thing" that "spoke all on its own" and haunted Derrida for years before the text was ever produced. "How can this fatally silent call that speaks before its own voice be made audible?" he asks. "How could it be kept waiting any longer?" (4). Derrida's response to this call is not to assert some sort of metaphysical authority but rather, and quite the contrary, to accede to "a studio of vocal writing" (6), "not in order to substitute the vocal setting for the book, but to give each of them their space or rather their *specific* volume, in such a way that each medium is affected or reinvented by the other" (5). In this process, the site of the voice becomes the site of "risk" and "decision" (5, 7), an "indetermination itself that makes the experience of the gramophonic act so perilous" (6). "At each syllable, even at each silence," Derrida writes, "a decision is imposed. . . . And what it signs is neither the law nor the truth" (7).

Derrida's term "gramophonic" reminds us that the voice is the site of "decision" precisely because it is the site of inscription. The fact of recording the polylogue doesn't stabilize and fix the voice but rather redoubles what was always already true about it, for as Derrida notes in "Ulysses Gramophone: Hear Say Yes in Joyce," "In order for the *yes* of affirmation"—in response, for example, to the "fatally silent call" of *il y a là cendre*—to be what it is, "it must carry the repetition within itself" of the trace to which it responds, and thus "we can already hear a gramophony which records writing in the liveliest voice."[5] And though, in the phrase *il y a là cendre*, "the resemblance sketched by this homophonic *là*, 'there,' made a feminine phantom tremble deep within the word," as Derrida puts it (15), he finally acknowledges that "they change sex, they re-cinder themselves, they androgynocide themselves" (43), not only because of the same "indecision between writing and voice" (4–5) we noted a moment ago, but also for the reasons that Derrida invokes when he quotes this passage from Nietzsche late in the text: "Our entire world is the *cinder* of innumerable *living* beings" (51).

Note that he does not say "living *human* beings." And in this context—namely, the vast body of Derrida's later work on the so-called question of "the animal"—the neat heteronormative binaries of sex and gender must give way to a much more complex and heterogeneous mode of thinking life and death, a context in which Derrida's later work exposes how the recourse to "animality" in the philosophical tradition has so often tethered heteronormative sexual identity to reproduction. In this light, Derrida's unwieldy neologism "androgynocide" anticipates and points us toward a properly biopolitical question

5. In *A Derrida Reader: Between the Blinds*, ed. Peggy Kamuf (New York: Columbia University Press, 1991), 576.

that nearly all commentary on Derrida, Judaism, and the Holocaust completely ignores: their complicated relationship to what Derrida fearlessly characterizes as a holocaust and "genocide" of nonhuman animals going on all around us, at every moment.[6] Later texts such as *The Animal That Therefore I Am* and *The Beast and Sovereign* seminars quite clearly develop the line of inquiry around Heidegger and human versus animal life begun in *Of Spirit*, but they do so in a way that allows us to return to that earlier text and read its biopolitical stakes anew, especially when we articulate them with later political writings of Derrida's such as *Rogues*. There, Derrida confronts but also radicalizes the question Hannah Arendt addressed in *The Origins of Totalitarianism* (a text we now view as part of the prehistory of what would come to be called biopolitical thought), where she feels the question of "the right to have rights" pressing against her conventionalist Aristotelian concept of the political.[7] Derrida writes,

Does democratic equality end at citizenship, and thus at the borders of the nation-state? Or must we extend it to the whole world of singularities, to the whole world of humans assumed to be like me, my compeers [*mes semblables*]— or else, even further, to all nonhuman living beings, or

6. Jacques Derrida, *The Animal That Therefore I Am*, ed. Marie-Louise Mallet, trans. David Wills (New York: Fordham University Press, 2008), 26. Further references are given in the text.

7. For more on Arendt and "the right to have rights," see my *Before the Law: Humans and Other Animals in a Biopolitical Frame* (Chicago: University of Chicago Press, 2013), 6–9.

again, even beyond that, to all the nonliving, to their memory, spectral or otherwise, to their to-come or to their indifference with regard to what we think we can identify, in an always precipitous, dogmatic, and obscure way, as the life or the living present of the living [la vivance] in general?[8]

These questions—the "like me" and "life" in relation to the supposed "living present of the living in general"—are changed decisively by the asystemacity of the cinder, which forces us to rethink them on the basis of a logic that is not essentially human, of which "what calls *itself* man" (*The Animal* 30) is in truth an epiphenomenon. Derrida tells us in this text that the cinder is "the best paradigm for the trace" and "not, as some have believed, and he as well, perhaps, the trail of the hunt, the fraying, the furrow in the sand, the wake in the sea, the love of the step for its imprint" (25). Now the trace, as we know, both "constitutes the self-presence of the living present" and "introduces into self-presence from the beginning all the impurity putatively excluded from it." It is thus "the intimate relation of the living present to its outside, the opening to exteriority in general"[9] that "impels us beyond present life . . . its empirical or ontological actuality: not toward death but toward a *living-on* [*sur-vie*] . . . of which

8. Jacques Derrida, *Rogues: Two Essays on Reason*, trans. Pascale-Anne Brault and Michael Naas (Stanford: Stanford University Press, 2005), 52. Further references are given in the text.
9. Jacques Derrida, *Speech and Phenomena*, trans. David B. Allison, in *A Derrida Reader*, 26–27.

life and death would themselves be but traces . . . a survival whose possibility in advance comes to disjoin or dis-adjust the identity to itself of the living present" (*Specters of Marx* 27–28, 65). But it is as if the enigmatic materiality of the cinder, more than these figures from human and animal life, or from nature, makes the cinder more trace than trace, as it were, its mark now even more inscrutable than the Derridean grapheme, as if the grapheme had collapsed in on itself, further compressing what Derrida calls "the becoming space of time" that it constitutes in its charred graphite crypt.[10] Thus the cinder, like the trace but even more than the trace, unsettles the "like me" and "life" of the "living present" because it is "extended to the entire field of the living," as Derrida puts it, *"or rather to the life/ death relation,* beyond the anthropological limits of 'spoken' language."[11]

So it is that we find in *"Il y a là cendre"* ("cinders there are") something that "comes to disjoin or dis-adjust the identity to itself of the living present." Here, as Lukacher notes, "the privative *a* takes the form of the silent difference between *la cendre* and *là cendre,* between 'the cinder' and 'there cinder.' In this telecommunicated signal, 'there' is precisely

10. On the grapheme, see Jacques Derrida, *Of Grammatology,* trans. Gayatri Chakravorty Spivak (Baltimore: Johns Hopkins University Press, 1976), 9, 84. Further references are given in the text.

11. "Violence against Animals," in *For What Tomorrow . . . : A Dialogue,* by Jacques Derrida and Elisabeth Roudinesco, trans. Jeff Fort (Stanford: Stanford University Press, 2004), 63, italics mine.

what oscillates," marked by the graphemic cinder, the accent, which in turn marks the "there" as part of the general economy of presence and absence that Derrida has written about from the very beginning, reinscribing it, in turn, in the difference between written and spoken language. And "there" is thus also the place of mourning, which, for these very same reasons, can never be reached, a mourning that can never achieve completion and for that reason still clings, interminably, to something still "there" ("Mourning Becomes Telepathy" 8, 12). But when you arrive "there" you will not find "him" or "them" or even "it"; you will find only cinders, the traces that remain, a "becoming-space of time" of which life and death are only traces. Likewise, the homonyms *feu* [fire] and *fut* [was] that Derrida crosses and superimposes in the text lead us to the (non)place of Derrida's assertion that the cinder is "what remains without remaining from the holocaust, from the all-burning, from the incineration" (25).

Here, then, a certain theory of the trace and of the cinder begins to shade into a certain politics of the trace and its formal dynamics—not of language per se (which is why Derrida reminds us that early in his work he substituted the concept of the trace for the concept of the signifier)[12] but a general economy of trace and cinder that clearly extends in Derrida's view to the question of (at least some)

12. See *The Animal That Therefore I Am*, 135.

nonhuman beings (but who knows *who*, as we have seen in *Rogues*, or how many?). To mention this fact is to unavoidably raise the question of "race" (in the heaviest scare quotation marks we can muster), because race and "racialization" have been the primary means under biopolitics for the "animalization" of human populations and their consequent exclusion from the *demos* (a connection clinched by Derrida's remarks on the holocaust and "genocide" of nonhuman animals in *The Animal That Therefore I Am*).

As Michel Foucault notes in his influential work on biopolitics, it is race that will "create caesuras within the biological continuum addressed by biopower," introducing "a break into the domain of life that is under power's control: the break between what must live and what must die."[13] More than this, Foucault argues that Nazism will bring to the breaking point the political logic that Derrida will explore in his later work (in *Rogues*, *Philosophy in a Time of Terror*, and the essay "Faith and Knowledge," among others) under the concept of "autoimmunity." Under Nazism, the immunitary logic of what Foucault calls "state racism" reaches its apotheosis only to flip over into the *auto*immunitary logic analyzed by Derrida. For Nazism, "the

13. Michel Foucault, *"Society Must Be Defended": Lectures at the Collège de France, 1975–1976*, ed. Mauro Bertani and Alessandro Fontana, trans. David Macey (New York: Picador, 2003), 254–55. Further references are in the text.

death of the other, the death of the bad race, of the inferior race (or the degenerate, or the abnormal), is something that will make life in general healthier: healthier and purer" (255), but only to give way to the *auto*immunitary drive whereby Hitler in Telegram 71 in April 1945, with Berlin under siege, gives the order to destroy the living conditions of the German people, who had proven themselves unworthy, precisely so that *Das Volk* of the Third Reich might be preserved (260). With Nazism, Foucault writes, "we have an absolutely racist State, an absolutely murderous State, and an absolutely suicidal State," but "this play," he argues, "is in fact inscribed in the workings of all States" of the modern form (260).

At stake in determining the political character of this violence is understanding not so much its ontological dimension but rather its formal mechanism—namely, whether or not it is a sacrificial form of violence (a topic that Derrida raises forcefully with regard to nonhuman beings in the interview "Eating Well" and his trenchant analysis of all those "carnophallogocentric" discourses that "do not sacrifice sacrifice," as he puts it).[14] Those questions in turn will illuminate decisively the entire biopolitical field into which we are attempting

14. Jacques Derrida, "'Eating Well,' or The Calculation of the Subject: An Interview with Jacques Derrida," in *Who Comes after the Subject?* ed. Eduardo Cadava, Peter Connor, and Jean-Luc Nancy (New York: Routledge, 1991), 113. Further references are in the text.

to insert the muted, indeed self-muting, text of *Cinders*—a field shaped in no small part by Derrida's complex relationship to Heidegger and how that differs from Giorgio Agamben's quite different Heideggerian commitments.

I say "muted and self-muting" because Derrida insists that the phrase "cinders there are" "thus says what it does, what it is. It immediately incinerates itself, in front of your eyes" (17)—only to immediately qualify that by observing that "I do not like this verb, 'to incinerate'; I find in it no affinity with the vulnerable tenderness, with the patience of a cinder. The verb is active, acute, incisive" (17). "To incinerate," in other words, already moves too quickly toward the self-confident and appropriative agency of what Derrida elsewhere calls the "auto-" that he has deconstructed in so many texts: of "autonomy," of the "autoaffection" of self-presence, of "man" as the "autobiographical animal," and so on (*The Animal* 24). For Derrida, all of these operate on the basis of a repression or denial of radical finitude, or what he will characterize as the "passivity" of a not-being-able (*The Animal* 27–28)—a finitude that is only redoubled for the very "human," as "auto-," who tries to escape it because, as I have argued elsewhere, it consists not just of our finitude as embodied beings who can experience suffering and privation but also of our subjection to the externality and *machinalité* of the trace as the very condition of possibility for "our" thoughts, "our" concepts, whatever they may be.[15] The "tenderness" and "patience" of this double finitude is part of what Derrida finds wanting in Heidegger's existential of "being-toward-death," which apparently acknowledges it but only to then reappropriate it for the "auto-" of the subject in a kind of carpe diem maneuver.[16] And this is why it is

> what is owed to the fire, and yet, if possible, without the shadow of a sacrifice, at noon, without debt, without the Phoenix, thus the unique phrase comes to set into place, in the place of no emplacement, the place solely of an incineration. The sentence ["cinders there are"] avows only the ongoing incineration, of which it remains the almost silent monument: this can be "there," là—(19)

As Lukacher rightly suggests, it is thus "the non-sacrificial nature of the Nazi Extermination that is silently at stake" in Cinders—not just in the selections from Glas that form the longest section of the "Animadversions," but also in the text's larger and most delicate effort to preserve the holocaust as "entirely other, nonpresent and outside the theorizable limits of ontology, leaving only the cinder traces of an absolute nonmemory" ("Mourning Becomes Telepathy" 13).

We can draw out how this bears on thinking questions of biopolitics by contrasting Derrida's

15. For a longer discussion of Derrida, passivity, the "auto-," and "double finitude," see my *What Is Posthumanism?* (Minneapolis: University of Minnesota Press, 2010), 81–95.

16. For an acute discussion of this point, see Richard Beardsworth, *Derrida and the Political* (London: Routledge, 1996), 130–31.

position here with Agamben's influential writings on the Holocaust and its political logic, but to do so we will also have to understand how this set of questions is, in turn, directly related to the opposing views these two hold on language, writing, speech, and finally law.[17] While a thorough comparison is beyond the scope of this Introduction, a few salient differences are worth noting to draw into focus the political stakes of Derrida's resistance to reading the Holocaust in terms of a sacrificial logic and how that resistance is directly related to his commitment to the figure of the trace cum cinder. As Jeffrey S. Librett notes, what Agamben resists above all in Derrida's work is precisely the trace, the cinder, writing in the sense of "arché-writing" as "limitless limitation and unending mediation" that prevents us "infinitely from gaining access to

17. Derrida's most direct encounter with Agamben's work takes place in the third session of *The Beast and Sovereign, Vol. 1*, trans. Geoffrey Bennington, ed. Michel Lisse, Marie-Louise Mallet, and Ginette Michaud (Chicago: University of Chicago Press, 2009). More oblique, though no less serious, is Derrida's assertion in *The Animal That Therefore I Am* regarding "*bios* and *zoe*, the biological, zoological, and anthropological," that "I would therefore hesitate just as much to say that we are living through a historical turning point. The figure of the turning point implies a rupture or an instantaneous mutation whose model or figure remains, precisely, to be questioned. As for history, historicity, even historicality, those motifs belonging precisely—as we shall see in detail—to *this* auto-definition, *this* auto-apprehension, *this* auto-situation of man or of the human *Dasein* as regards what is living and animal life; they belong to this auto-biography of man, which I wish to call into question today" (24). These points are amplified, and not without some humor, in Derrida's engagement of Agamben in the third session of *The Beast and the Sovereign, Vol. 1*.

the full presence (of the voice), separating us from our own Being and its meaning."[18] While Agamben's position advertises quite unabashedly its Heideggerian commitments, as Librett notes, it is also "powerfully and explicitly overdetermined by Christian thinking, in the Pauline tradition, as the metaphysics that poses God qua logos by polemicizing in favor of the living spirit (spirit as life), against the 'dead letter' of the law" (15). As Agamben puts it, following Paul in Corinthians, "The content of revelation is not a truth that can be expressed in the form of linguistic propositions about a being (even about a supreme being) but is, instead, a truth that concerns language itself, the very fact that language (and therefore knowledge) exists. . . . The invisibility of the revealer in what is revealed is the word of God; it is revelation" (qtd. Librett 15). In a word—if we may be permitted the expression in this context—Agamben thus establishes "a profound continuity between Pauline Christianity and the Heideggerian thinking of Being" (16), with "voice"—prior to meaning and mediation by the "dead" letter of writing—as what Agamben calls "the most universal dimension of meaning: Being" (qtd. 16). If, for Agamben, Holocaust testimony is the supreme instance of "the speaking of speech, the taking-place of language,"

18. Jeffrey S. Librett, "From the Sacrifice of the Letter to the Voice of Testimony: Giorgio Agamben's Fulfillment of Metaphysics," *Diacritics* 37: 2–3 (Summer–Fall 2007): 15. Further references are given in the text.

then by his own logic the destruction of the Jews in the Holocaust becomes "the revelation of poetic speech as a manifestation of the absolute." And so, in Librett's words, "unwittingly, Agamben ends up participating in the very kind of theodicy he ostensibly wished to avoid by denying the sacrificial character of the Holocaust in the first place" (12).

To get a sense of just how much is at stake here we should recall Derrida's discussion of Benjamin, the "Final Solution," and "divine" vs. "mythic" violence in the "Post-scriptum" to the essay "Force of Law." As Robert Eaglestone notes, Derrida here imagines that Benjamin would reject as irrelevant any judgment or trial or historiography of Nazism and the Holocaust that is "homogeneous with the space in which Nazism developed."[19] That is to say (and Derrida would agree) that judging the Holocaust is not about arguments over historical "fact," what did or did not happen and where, who knew and who did not, and so on. As Eaglestone puts it, from Benjamin's point of view, "Only that which is truly outside Nazism and the Final Solution could judge it or measure its significance." But it is precisely here that Derrida locates something "intolerable" in this interpretation. If "only a God can explain this," if the Holocaust, as Derrida puts it, is an "uninterpretable manifestation

19. Derrida quoted in Robert Eaglestone, "Derrida and the Holocaust: A Commentary on the Philosophy of Cinders," *Angelaki* 7: 2 (August 2002): 34. Further references are given in the text.

of divine violence," then one must be terrified, he concludes, "at the idea of an interpretation that would make of the Holocaust an expiation and an indecipherable signature of the just and violent anger of God."[20] And it is precisely here that Derrida finds Benjamin, and would find Agamben (and for the same reasons), "too Heideggerian, too messianco-Marxist, or too archeo-eschatalogical for me" (qtd. Eaglestone 34).

The stakes of this difference between Derrida and Agamben in the contemporary context of biopolitical thought may be further amplified. First, in light of Agamben's reinscription of the quite conventional idea that "the letter of (Jewish) law kills, while the spirit of the (Christian) revelations gives life" (Librett 17), Derrida may be said to be writing, quintessentially, "as" a Jew, but a Jew always already divided against himself, always already circumcised, as it were, and for that reason all the more "Jewish"—a fact thematized by his well-known autobiographical reminiscences about his unease and impatience with being raised "Jewish" and being forced to attend a Jewish school as a child, his status as an Algerian Jew, by the fact (to borrow Gil Anidjar's subtitle) of "Derrida, the Arab, the Jew," as itself a redoubling of the divided

20. Jacques Derrida, "Force of Law: The 'Mystical Foundation of Authority,'" trans. Mary Quaintance, in *Deconstruction and the Possibility of Justice*, ed. Drucilla Cornell, Michael Rosenfeld, and David Gray Carlson (New York: Routledge, 1992), 62. Qtd. in Eaglestone, 34.

and divisive character of the "Abrahamic" register in which Derrida writes about religion.[21] Further, as Geoffrey Bennington observes, "It is easy to imagine a scenario which would appropriate Derrida for a Jewish thought in some way opposed to a tyranny of the Greek *logos*, for a thinking of the law opposed to (or at least unassimilable by) a thought of Being."[22] On this view, Derrida is like the Jew for Hegel who

> remains under the sign of the cut: cut off from and in opposition to the community and love with Abraham, condemning himself to wandering in the desert outside any fixed domicile, marking this cut with the sign of circumcision to remain attached to the cut itself, subject as a finite

21. Gil Anidjar, "Introduction. 'Once More, Once More': Derrida, the Arab, the Jew," in *Acts of Religion*, ed. Gil Anidjar (New York: Routledge, 2002), 1, 3–4. With regard to the invocation of both Benjamin and Judaism, we should remember that all of what we are discussing can be repositioned against the backdrop, as it were, of Agamben's recruitment of Benjamin against Derrida in Agamben's disagreement with Derrida in chapter 4 of *Homo Sacer* over the meaning of Kafka's text "Before the Law." As Librett characterizes it, when Scholem and Benjamin debate the meaning of this text, "Scholem's all-too-Jewish, or 'bad' (traditionalist), reading loses out to Benjamin's not-too-Jewish, or 'good' Jewish (messianic), reading. And also not surprisingly, Agamben positions Derrida's reading as a version of Scholem's, while he advances his own as a version of Benjamin's. Benjamin plays here the role of the almost Christian Jew, the one who is rigorously opposed to (Jewish) legalism and the one who correspondingly objects to the opacity of the letter" (22). Derrida's most frontal engagement with Agamben occurs (with humor) in the third session of *The Beast and the Sovereign, Vol. 1*.

22. Geoffrey Bennington and Jacques Derrida, *Jacques Derrida*, trans. Geoffrey Bennington (Chicago: University of Chicago Press, 1993), 293. Further references are in the text.

being to the infinite power of a jealous God from whom he cuts himself. . . . The Jew is alienated, in a relation not with a transcendent truth but with a transcendent which takes the (formless) form of the command and the incomprehensible law—which cannot therefore be rational—but which one undergoes without mediation in its letter and not its spirit. (294–95)

But as Bennington notes, "Such a schema, with everything that might be satisfying about it, would stumble somewhere on the relation of Derrida to Heidegger, which one might be tempted to describe as aberrant, or even pathological" (293–94)—would stumble, that is, on what Derrida calls a certain "Heideggerian intention" that underlies the idea of the trace, signifying, "sometimes beyond Heideggerian discourse," as he puts it, "the undermining of an ontology which, in its innermost course, has determined the meaning of being as presence and the meaning of language as the full continuity of speech" (Of Grammatology 70).

For our purposes, the "aberrant, or even pathological" character of this "Heideggerian intention" would be not so much that Derrida's concept of the trace "follows through" on the philosophical project inaugurated by Heidegger, radicalizing via the "spacing" of the trace the relations of presence and absence already nascently at work in Heidegger's argument that Being is not "present" (that Being is time) but rather that it does so on the terrain of both race/species and flame/Holocaust. With regard to the former, while Derrida takes issue with Heidegger's assertion that the animal "has a world in the mode of not having," because it supposedly does not "have access to entities *as such* and in their Being," which in turn "derives from the properly *phenomenological* impossibility of speaking the phenomenon" (*Of Spirit* 53), he at the same time extends the "Heideggerian intention" underneath the trace to nonhuman animals. As he argues in "Eating Well," the "possibilities or necessities" of "the mark in general, of the trace, of iterability, of *différance*," "without which there would be no language, *are themselves not only human,*" which thus "does not allow us to 'cut' once and for all where we would in general like to cut" (116–17). Indeed, as I have argued elsewhere—more "aberrantly" or "pathologically" still—if this is the case, and if the trace is the simultaneous condition of possibility and impossibility for conceptualization and cognition as such, then (ironically enough) Heidegger's description of animals as "having a world in the mode of not having" is as good a definition of *Dasein*—animal *or* human—as we are likely to get.[23] All of which is to say that there is no "*the* Jew" just as there is no "*the* Animal," and for the same reasons: reasons that, "pathologically" enough, "continue" to be Heideggerian in the precise sense that Derrida invokes when he asserts that he, *with* Heidegger, rejects what he calls

23. See my *Before the Law,* 80.

"biologistic continuism" whose "sinister connotations" include the naturalization of racism, xenophobia, Social Darwinism, and so on.[24]

This inability "to 'cut' once and for all where we would in general like to cut" decisively changes the character of the biopolitical in ways that are heterogeneous to the logic of sacrifice—and heterogeneous too to the clear-cut distinctions between friend and enemy that are crucial to securing a concept of the "properly" political in the writings of Carl Schmitt, whose work is, in turn, of signal importance to Agamben's rendering of biopolitics in his book *State of Exception*.[25] For Derrida, all such attempts to cordon off a "proper" domain (of the political,

24. *The Animal*, 30. On this topic, see as well *Of Spirit*, where Derrida writes that Heidegger's "humanist teleology" of *weltbildend*, *Dasein*, and so on, "in spite of all the denegations or all the avoidances one could wish . . . has remained *up till now* (in Heidegger's time and situation, but this has not radically changed today) the price to be paid in the ethico-political denunciation of biologism, racism, naturalism, etc." (56). For even more on Derrida's "aberrant, or even pathological" relation to Heidegger, see, for example, Derrida's complex circumnavigations, over a nearly twenty-year period, of the late Heidegger's concept of *Zusage* and how it rewrites or unwrites (if that is how we want to put it) concepts in Heidegger such as "being" and "spirit." For an overview of this set of investigations as related in turn to what Derrida in *The Animal That Therefore I Am* (quoting himself in a footnote from *Of Spirit*) calls "the gnawing, ruminant, and silent voracity" of "an animal-machine of reading and rewriting," see my *Before the Law*, 80–82.

25. See Giorgio Agamben, *State of Exception*, trans. Kevin Attell (Chicago: University of Chicago Press, 2005). Derrida has much to say about Schmitt and his friend/enemy distinction in both *The Beast and the Sovereign, Vol. 1* and *The Politics of Friendship*, trans. George Collins (London: Verso, 2005).

of "language" or "speech," of "man," of "the Jew," and even of "the Holocaust") are doomed to failure and always will, and more importantly, threaten to rebound back on those who insist on maintaining such "immunitary" zones of identity—all of which Derrida returns to time and again in his later writings on (auto)immunity, democracy, hospitality, and justice.

The final biopolitical consequence I want to draw out of Derrida's position on sacrificial violence and the (auto)immunity secured by it (a linkage pursued in detail in the late essay "Faith and Knowledge")[26] may be glimpsed by returning one last time to the Abrahamic *topos* on which Derrida writes about religion and sacrifice, with David Wills's observation that, for Derrida, "not only is Abraham's action ethically untenable, it is criminal." And yet, he notes, for Derrida it would be an even more serious crime to think that it is an exception, an "aberration" or "marginal practice" that has nothing to do with us. Quite the contrary, Wills writes, for Derrida "society is founded upon the enactment of criminal sacrifice." Hence the "monotonous complacency," as Derrida puts it, of "discourses on morality, politics, and the law, and the exercise of its rights (whether private, public, national, or international)," that are

26. Jacques Derrida, "Faith and Knowledge: Two Sources of 'Religion' at the Limits of Reason Alone," trans. Samuel Weber, in *Religion*, ed. Jacques Derrida and Gianni Vattimo (Stanford: Stanford University Press, 1998).

in no way impaired by the fact that, because of the structures of the laws of the market that society has instituted and controls, because of the mechanisms of external debt and other similar inequities, that same "society" *puts to death* or . . . *allows* to die of hunger and disease tens of millions of children (those neighbors or fellow humans that ethics or the discourse of the rights of man refer to) without any moral or legal tribunal ever being considered competent to judge such a sacrifice, the sacrifice of others to avoid being sacrificed oneself. Not only is it true that such a society participates in this incalculable sacrifice, it actually organizes it. The smooth functioning of its economic, political, and legal affairs, the smooth functioning of its moral discourse and good conscience presupposes the permanent operation of this sacrifice.[27]

Here we find—to make the point canonically, as it were—what Foucault famously characterizes as the fundamental qualitative shift from sovereignty to biopolitics. While the former "took life and let live," the latter "consists in making live and letting die" (*"Society Must Be Defended"* 247). But Derrida's crucial intervention in the biopolitical field is that he forces on us a question never quite broached, as Donna Haraway and others have noted, in Foucault's analysis of biopolitics, which discloses the crucial function of race in introducing "caesuras"

27. David Wills, *Matchbook: Essays in Deconstruction* (Stanford: Stanford University Press, 2005), 117. The passage quoted from Derrida is from *The Gift of Death*, 85–86, qtd. here 117–18. See also in this connection *Philosophy in a Time of Terror: Dialogues with Jürgen Habermas and Jacques Derrida*, ed. Giovanna Borradori (Chicago: University of Chicago Press, 2003), 107–9.

in the "biological continuum" that allow a life to be killable but not murderable, only then to stop at the water's edge of species difference.[28] But for Derrida, what is "owed to the flame" is no such certainty about "what we think we can identify, in an always precipitous, dogmatic, and obscure way, as the life or the living present of living [*la vivance*] in general." Or to put it in terms not of "life" but of "race," the "Jews" of Foucault's analysis of Nazi biopolitics are not "Algerian" enough. For when Derrida writes, "I shall speak of ghost [*revenant*], of flame, and of ashes," we are forced to say, "yes, but whose? And where, if not here?"

28. See Donna J. Haraway, *When Species Meet* (Minneapolis: University of Minnesota Press, 2008), 59–60.

Cinders

More than fifteen years ago a phrase came to me, as though in spite of me; to be more precise, it returned, unique, uniquely succinct, almost mute. I thought I had calculated it cunningly, mastered and overwhelmed it, as if I had appropriated it once and for all.
Since then, I have repeatedly had to yield to the evidence: the phrase dispensed with all authorization; she had lived without me.
She, the phrase, had always lived alone.
The first time (was it the first time?), more than fifteen years ago, at the end of a book, *Dissemination*, in the acknowledgments, where a book is dedicated, offered, rendered up to those who, known or unknown, have already given it to you in advance, the sentence in question imposed itself on me with the authority, so discreet and simple it was, of a judgment: "there are cinders there," "cinders there are" [*il y a là cendre*].
Là written with an accent grave: *là*, there, cinder there is, there is, there, cinder. But the accent, although readable to the eye, is not heard: cinder

3

there is. To the ear, the definite article, *la,* risks effacing the place, and any mention or memory of the place, the adverb *là* . . . But read silently, it is the reverse: *là* effaces *la, la* effaces herself, himself, twice rather than once.

This sentence, in which each letter had a secret meaning for me, I used again later, whether a citation or not, in other texts: *Glas, The Postcard,* for example.

For nearly ten years, this specter's comings and goings, unforeseen visits of the ghost. The thing spoke all on its own. I had to explain myself to it, respond to it—or for it.

When some friends, in 1980, invited me to write on the theme of cinders for *Anima,* a now defunct journal, I proposed, in the parodied genre of the polylogue, an apparently unpronounceable conversation, really a writing apparatus that, one might say, *called* to the voice, to voices. But how can this fatally silent call that speaks before its own voice be made audible? How could it be kept waiting any longer?

In effect two pieces of writing come face to face on the page: on the righthand side, the polylogue proper, an entanglement of an indeterminate number of voices, of which some seem masculine, others feminine, and this is sometimes marked in the grammar of the sentence. These readable grammatical signs disappear for the most part when spoken aloud, which aggravates a certain indecision between writing and voice, an indecision already risked by the word *là*, with or without the accent, in "there are cinders there," "cinders there are."

This tension risked between writing and speech, this vibration of grammar in the voice, is one of the themes of the polylogue. And this polylogue, it seems, is destined for the eye; it corresponds only to an interior voice, an absolutely low voice.

But precisely thereby [*par là*] the polylogue engaged reading; it analyzed perhaps what vocalization [*mise en voix*] could call forth and at the same time risk losing, an impossible utterance and undiscoverable tonalities. Will I dare to say that my desire had a place, its place, between this call and this risk? What was it waiting for?

Then one day came the possibility, I should say the chance of making a tape recording of this. Before the technical means (which themselves mark a moment of singular innovation in the history of publishing), this opportunity presupposes the desire, here that of Antoinette Fouque: to breach a way into the voices at work in a body of writing. And in short, to situate them in the work, indeed to put them to work. Not in order to substitute the vocal setting for the book, but to give to each of them their space or rather their *specific* volume, in such a way that each medium is affected or reinvented by the other. I do not believe that silent reading will suffer from this, nor will the book's desire, which, on the contrary, receives new interpretive impetus from this experiment. Des Femmes proposes not only this double medium, printed page and tape recording, from here on indissociable in their very heterogeneity, but also provides a place for it, a sort of research laboratory, a studio of vocal writing, in which an interpretive experiment becomes possible.

On what experiment have we embarked together, Michèle Muller, Carole Bouquet, and myself? We have put this question to the test, at once fearful and defiant: under what conditions does one take the risk of vocalization, the very act I had awaited, having already described it, given notice of it, above all dreaded it as the impossible itself, some would say the "prohibited" [*l'interdit*]? On the page it is as though each word were chosen, then placed in such a way that nothing uttered by any voice could gain access to it.

In certain cases, in the absence of indications to the contrary, it is the indetermination itself that makes the experience of the gramophonic act so perilous: too much freedom, a thousand ways, all just as legitimate, to accentuate, to set the rhythm, to make the tone change.

In other cases, where it is still a question of caesura, pause or agreement, the most contradictory decisions were required simultaneously: the same syllable should be pronounceable on two incompatible registers—but then again it shouldn't be. This potentiality remains, so to speak, in the background [*dans le fond*], to be perceived by silent reading precisely as something enveloped, veiled. How can we force this potentiality out of hiding without an act of faith, the absolute hiatus at the moment of an impossible decision? This decision is always confided, when the time comes, to the other's voice. No, to *a voice* of the other, to another voice: here, that of Carole Bouquet.

Who will decide whether this voice was lent, returned, or given? And to whom?

By entangling itself in impossible choices, the spoken "recorded" voice makes a reservoir of writing readable, its tonal and phonic drives, the waves (neither cry nor speech) that are knotted or unknotted in the unique vociferation, the singular range of another voice. This voice, to narrow the possibilities, is then left to pass away, it has passed away in advance, doubly present memory or doubly divided presence.

What is involved in this phonographic act? Here's an interpretation, one among others. At each syllable, even at each silence, a decision is imposed: it was not always deliberate or sometimes even the same from one repetition to the other. And what it signs is neither the law nor the truth. Other interpretations remain possible—and doubtless necessary. Thus we analyze the resource this double text affords us today: on the one hand, a graphic space opened to multiple readings, in the traditional and protected form of the book (and it is not like a prompt-book, because each time it gives a different reading, another gift, dealing out a new hand all over again), but on the other hand, simultaneously, and also for the first time, we have the tape recording of a singular interpretation, made one day, by so on and so forth, at a single stroke calculated and by chance.

To decide, sometimes without wanting to, between several interpretations (in the sense of reading that is also that of music and theater): the voice does not betray a text. If it did, it would be in the sense that betrayal is a revelation; for example, the restless polylogue that divides up each atom of writing. Manifestation of the impossible truth on which it will have been necessary to decide once and for all, at every instant, and despite repetitions. The utterance thus betrays; it unveils what will have, one day, carried it away, between the divisions of all the voices or those into which the same voice divides itself.

Facing the polylogue, on the lefthand page, quotations from other texts *(Dissemination, Glas, The Postcard)*[1] that all say something about the cinder, mingle their ashes and the word *cendre* with something else. The quotations co-appear along with it, they are "summoned" [*comparaissent*]:

1. Although it is not cited, another text is alluded to: "Télépathie," a kind of supplement to *The Postcard*, which, like *Glas*, is woven around the letters LAC, CLA, ALC, CAL, ACL, and so on (*Furor* 2 [1981] and *Confrontation* 10 [1983]). *Schibboleth* (1986), also dedicated to cinders, was not yet published.

an incomplete archive, still burning or already consumed, recalling certain textual sites, the continuous, tormenting, obsessive meditation about what are and are not, what is meant or silenced by, cinders. These quotations are titled here "Animadversions," which in Latin means "observations," "perceptions," or "calls to attention," and which I chose in homage to the journal *Anima*.

Finally, may I emphasize two difficulties among others in the resonant scenography that was attempted elsewhere. To begin with, it was necessary at once to mark and efface the accent on *à* in *là* in *il y a là cendre* and elsewhere. To do both at once was impossible, and if the word *accent* says something about *song*, it is the experience of cinders and song that here seeks its name.

So if the recorded version makes two voices heard, of which one seems masculine, the other feminine, that does not reduce the polylogue to a duet, much less to a duel. And the effect of mentioning "another voice," which one sometimes hears without reading it, will often be to put one on one's guard. It signals that each of the two voices yields to still others. I repeat, they are indeterminate in number: the voice of the signatory of the texts is the figure of only one among others, and it is not certain whether this figure is masculine, or whether the other is a woman.

But the words "another voice" recall not only the complex multiplicity of people, they "call," they "ask for" another voice: "another voice, again, yet another voice." It is a desire, an order, a prayer or a promise, as you wish: "another voice, may it come soon now, again, another voice . . ." An order or a promise, the desire of a prayer, I don't know, not yet.

J. D.

CINDERS

Animadversions

I

*"Moving off of itself, forming itself wholly therein, almost
without remainder, writing denies and recognizes its debt
in a single dash. The utmost disintegration of the signature,
far from the center, indeed from the secrets that are shared
there, divided up so as to scatter even their ashes.*
*"Though the letter gains strength solely from this in-
direction, and granted that it can always not arrive at the
other side, I will not use this as a pretext to absent myself
from the punctuality of a dedication: R. Gasché, J. J. Goux,
J. C. Lebensztejn, J. H. Miller, others, there are cinders there,
cinders there are* [il y a là cendre], *will recognize, perhaps,
what their reading has contributed here.* December 1971.*"*

— And near the end, at the bottom of the last page, it was as though you had signed with these words: "There are cinders there," "Cinders there are." I read, reread them; it was so simple, and yet I knew that I was not there; without waiting for me the phrase withdrew into its secret.

— All the more because this word, *là*, "there," you would no longer let it be heard. Listening only to it, with eyes closed, I liked putting my mind at rest by whispering "the cinder," confusing this *là*, "there," yes, with *la*, the singular feminine definite article. It was necessary to decipher without losing equilibrium between the eye and the ear; I am not sure that I could prevent it.

— As for me, I had at first imagined that cinders were there, not here but there, as a story to be told: cinder, this old gray word, this dusty theme of humanity, the immemorial image had decomposed from within, a metaphor or metonymy of itself, such is the destiny of every cinder, separated, consumed like a cinder of cinders. Who would still dare run the risk of a poem of the cinder? One might dream that the word *cinder* was itself a cinder in that sense, "there," "over there," in the distant past, a lost memory of what is no longer here. And thereby *[par là]* its phrase would have meant, without holding anything back: the cinder is no longer here. Was *[fut]* it ever?

13

— There are cinders there, cinders there are; when that happened *[fut]* nearly ten years ago the phrase withdrew from itself. The phrase carried distance within itself, within herself. Despite its venue and despite all appearances, it did not permit itself, did not permit herself, to sign; it no longer belonged; somewhat as if, signifying nothing that was *[fût]* intelligible, the phrase came from very far away to meet its supposed signatory, who did not even read it, who scarcely received it, dreamed it rather, like a legend or a saying, a whiff of tobacco smoke: these words that leave your mouth only to be lost in unrecognizability.

— Just suppose, this is what I would have liked to ask (but to whom?). This morning, for the first time, ten years later, I became aware to the point of being able to admit to myself that something about this reading is imprinted in me, in a place sheltered but ready for silent ecstasy: the article missing before such cinders, in a word, the resemblance sketched by this homophonic *là*, "there," made a feminine phantom tremble deep within the word, in the smoke, the proper name deep within the common noun. The cinder is not here, but there is the Cinder there.

— Who is Cinder? Where is she? Where did she run off to at this hour? If the homophony withholds the singular name within the common noun, it was surely "there," *là*, someone vanished but something preserved her trace and at the same time lost it, the

15

16

cinder. There the cinder is: that which preserves in order no longer to preserve, dooming the remnant to dissolution. And it is no longer the one who has disappeared who leaves cinders "there"; it is only her still unreadable name. And nothing prevents us from thinking that this may also be the nickname of the so-called signatory. There are cinders there, cinders there are, the phrase thus says what it does, what it is. It immediately incinerates itself, in front of your eyes: an impossible mission (but I do not like this verb, "to incinerate"; I find in it no affinity with the vulnerable tenderness, with the patience of a cinder. The verb is active, acute, incisive).

— No, the phrase does not say what it is, but what it was [fut], and since this vocable was [fut] just used by you so many times, do not forget that it remains in memory of the departed [feu], of the word feu in the idiom, "the late so and so," the departed, the bereaved. Cinder of all our lost etymologies, fatum, fuit, functus, defunctus.

— The sentence says what it will have been, from the moment it gives itself up to itself, giving itself as its own proper name, the consumed (and consummate) art of the secret: of knowing how to keep itself from showing.

— Just suppose, I would have asked, that this saying only gives a signal and only in order to say nothing other than itself: I am a cinder signal, I recall

something or someone of whom I will say nothing but this rough sketch obviously in order to say that nothing will have had to annul what is said in its saying, to give it to the fire, to destroy it in the flame, and not otherwise. No cinder without fire *[feu]*.

That is what is owed to the fire, and yet, if possible, without the shadow of a sacrifice, at noon, without debt, without the Phoenix, thus the unique phrase comes to set into place, in the place of no emplacement, the place solely of an incineration. The sentence avows only the ongoing incineration, of which it remains the almost silent monument: this can be "there," *là*—

— But why would you have given it to the fire? To preserve the hiddenness of mourning's ashen grayness, or to undo it by letting it be seen, the half-mourning that persists only as long as the time of a cinder? Why cinders "there"? The place of burning, but of what, of whom? As long as one does not know, and you will never know, the sentence says what it said earlier, the incinerated is no longer nothing, nothing but the cinder, the innermost cinder furnace, a remnant that must no longer remain, this place of nothing that may be, a pure place was marked out.

— Pure is the word. It calls for fire. There are cinders there, cinders there are, this is what takes place in letting a place occur, so that it will be understood:

19

Nothing will have taken place but the place. Cinders there are: Place there is [il y a lieu].

— Where? Here? There? Where are the words on a page?

— There are prescribed limits. The idiom *il y a lieu*, you will never translate it, no more than you will a hidden proper name, for this is what carries everything away: toward the recognition, the debt, the obligation, the prescribed limit. There is a place for this, there is good reason for this, a proper name, place there is for doing this or that, for giving, rendering, celebrating, loving. And because of this, the locality of the legend ("cinders there are") surrounds it with friendship, bestowing grace and dissemination at the same time. There are cinders there, that was [fut] finally like the fragile, singed, and crumbling title of the book *Dissemination*. Discreetly pushed to the side, dissemination thus expresses in five words [il y a là cendre] what is destined, by the fire, to dispersion without return, the pyrification of what does not remain and returns to no one.

— If a place is itself surrounded by fire (falls finally to ash, into a cinder tomb), it no longer is. Cinder remains, cinder there is, which we can translate: the cinder is not, is not what is. It remains *from* what is not, in order to recall at the delicate, charred bottom of itself only nonbeing or nonpresence. Being without presence has not been and will no longer

be there where there is cinder and where this other memory would speak. There, where cinder means the difference between what remains and what is, will she ever reach it, there?

— Perhaps he finds it unseemly to have to comment, even to read and to cite this phrase: he is, in effect, "really incensed" at having, in a word, "to incense" it. Regardless what he may say, "there are cinders there" remains his. And everything we will say and advance here about it, concerning the legal signature that he pretends to undermine, he will reinstate it, he will take it back again, will give it to the hearth of its own burning—or of its own family. There are cinders only insofar as there is the hearth, the fireplace, some fire or place. Cinder as the house of being . . .

— Your precaution is naive. He will answer however he chooses. While the phrase appears in a book bearing his signature, it does not belong to him. He admits having already read it before writing it, before writing her. She, this cinder, was given or lent to him by so many others, through so much forgetting, and besides, no one here flatters this secret with a commentary. We literally unveil nothing of her, nothing that in the final account does not leave her intact, virginal (that's the only thing he loves), undecipherable, impassively tacit, in a word, sheltered from the cinder that there is and that she is. For abandoned to its solitude, witness to whomever

II

"Pure and figureless, this light burns all. It burns itself in the all-burning [le brule-tout] it is, leaves, of itself or anything, no trace, no mark, no sign of passage. Pure consuming destruction, pure effusion of light without shadow, noon without contrary, without resistance, without obstacle, waves, showers, streams ablaze with light: '[. . .] (Lichtgüsse) [. . .].'"

"The all-burning is 'an essenceless by-play, pure accessory of the substance that rises without ever setting (ein wesenloses Beiherspielen an dieser Substanz die nur aufgeht, ohne in sich niederzugehen), without becoming a subject, and without consolidating through the self (Selbst) its differences.'"

or whatever, the sentence does not even say the cinder. This thing of which one knows nothing, knows neither what past is still carried in these gray dusty words, nor what substance came to consume itself there before extinguishing itself there (do you know how many types of cinders the naturalists distinguish? and for what "wood" such cinders sometimes recall a desire?); will one still say of such a thing that it even preserves the identity of a cinder? At present, here and now, there is something material—visible but scarcely readable—that, referring only to itself, no longer makes a trace, unless it traces only by losing the trace it scarcely leaves

— that it just barely remains

— but that is just what he calls the trace, this effacement. I have the impression now that the best paradigm for the trace, for him, is not, as some have believed, and he as well, perhaps, the trail of the hunt, the fraying, the furrow in the sand, the wake in the sea, the love of the step for its imprint, but the cinder (what remains without remaining from the holocaust, from the all-burning, from the incineration the incense)

— That it remains for very few people, and, however slightly one touches it, it falls, it does not fall into cinders, it gets lost down to the cinder of its cinders. In writing this way, he burns one more time, he burns what he still adores although he has already burned it, he is intent on it

25

"... fire artist. The word itself (Beiherspielen) plays the example (Beispiel) beside the essence."

"The all-burning—that has taken place once and nonetheless repeats itself ad infinitum—diverges so well from all essential generality that it resembles the pure difference of an absolute accident. Play and pure difference, those are the secret of an imperceptible all-burning, the torrent of fire that sets itself ablaze. Letting itself get carried away, pure difference is different from itself, therefore indifferent. The pure play of difference is nothing, does not even relate to its own conflagration. The light envelops itself in darkness even before becoming subject."

"How, from this consuming destruction without limit, can there remain something that primes the dialectical process and opens history?"

"How would the purest of the pure, the worst of the worst, the panic blaze of the all-burning, put forth some monument, even were it a crematory? Some stable, geometric, solid form, for example, a pyramis that guards the trace of death? Pyramis is also a cake of honey and flour. It was offered as a reward for a sleepless night to the one who thus remained awake."

"If the all-burning destroys up to its letter and its body, how can it guard the trace of itself and breach/broach a history where it preserves itself in losing itself?"

Here is experienced the implacable force of sense, of mediation, of the hard-working negative. In order to be what it is, purity of play, of difference, of consuming destruction, the all-burning must pass into its contrary, guard itself, guard its own monument of loss, appear as what it is in its very disappearance. As soon as it appears, as soon as the fire shows itself, it remains, it keeps hold of itself, it loses itself as fire. Pure difference, different from (it)self, ceases to be what it is in order to remain what it is. That is the origin of history, the

beginning of the going down [déclin], *the setting of the sun,*
the passage to occidental subjectivity. Fire becomes for-(it)
self and is lost; yet worse [pire] *since better.*

Then in place of burning all, one begins to love flowers.
The religion of flowers follows the religion of the sun.

The erection of the pyramid guards life—the dead—in
order to give rise [donner lieu] *to the for-(it)self of adoration.*
This has the signification of a sacrifice, of an offer by which
the all-burning annuls itself, opens the annulus, contracts the
annulus into the anniversary of the solar revolution in sacri-
ficing itself as the all-burning, therefore in guarding itself."

"*The chance of substance, of the remnance* [restance]
determined as subsistence."

"*The difference and the play of the pure light, the panic*
and pyromaniac dissemination, the all-burning offers itself
as a holocaust to the for-(it)self, gibt sich dem Fürsichsein
zum Opfer. *It sacrifices itself, but only to remain, to ensure*
its guarding, to bind itself to itself strictly, to become itself,
for-(it)self, (close)-by-(it)self. In order to sacrifice itself, it
burns itself."

"*A panic, limitless inversion: the word* holocaust *that*
happens to translate Opfer *is more appropriate to the text*
than the word of Hegel himself. In this sacrifice, all (holos)
is burned (caustos), *and the fire can go out only stoked."*

"*What puts itself in play in this holocaust of play itself?"*

This perhaps: the gift, the sacrifice, the putting into
play or the setting on fire of everything, the holocaust
contains the seeds of ontology. Without the holocaust the
dialectical movement and the history of Being could not
open themselves, engage themselves in the annulus of
their anniversary, could not annul themselves in producing
the solar course from Orient to Occident. Before, if one
could count here with time, before everything, before every
determinable being [étant], *there is, there was, there will*

have been the irruptive event of the gift [don]. *An event that no more has any relation with what is currently designated under this word. Thus giving can no longer be thought starting from Being* [être], *but 'the contrary,' it could be said, if this logical inversion here were pertinent when the question is not yet logic but the origin of logic. In* Zeit und Sein, *the gift of the* es gibt *gives itself to be thought before the* Sein *in the* es gibt Sein *and displaces all that is determined under the name* Ereignis, *a word translated by* event." *[. . .]*

". . . *the process of the gift (before exchange), the process that is not a process but a holocaust, a holocaust of the holocaust,* engages *the history of Being but does not belong to it. The gift is* not; *the holocaust is* not; *if at least* something there is [il y en a]. *But as soon as it burns (the blaze is not a being) it must, burning itself, burn its very act of burning and begin to be. This reflection (in both senses of the word) of the holocaust engages history, the dialectic of sense, ontology, the speculative. The speculative is the reflection* (speculum) *of the holocaust's holocaust, the blaze reflected and cooled by the glass, the ice, of the mirror."* [. . .]

"A fatum *of the gift there is* [Il y a là], *and this necessity was said in the 'must'* (muss, doit) *we indicated above [. . .]. I give you—a pure gift, without exchange, without return—but whether I want this or not, the gift guards itself, keeps itself, and from then on you must owe* [tu dois]. [. . .] *The gift can only be a sacrifice, that is the axiom of speculative reason. Even if it upsurges 'before' philosophy and religion, the gift has for its destination or determination, for its* Bestimmung, *a return to self in philosophy, religion's truth."*

and I sense it,
I mean the odor of the body, perhaps his. All these
cinders, he feels them burning in his flesh.

— One says "warm cinders," "cold cinders,"
depending whether the fire still lingers there or no
longer stirs. But there? Where the cinder within a
sentence has for consistency only its syntax and for
body only its vocabulary? Does this make the words
warm or cold? Neither warm nor cold. And the gray
form of these letters? Between black and white, the
color of writing resembles the only "literality" of
the cinder that still inheres in a language. In a cinder of words, in the cinder of a name, the cinder
itself, the literal—that which he loves—has disappeared. The name "cinder" is still a cinder of the
cinder itself.

— That is why the cinder in a sentence here no longer is, but there is cinder there.

— There, *là*, an incineration of the definite article
leaves the cinder itself in cinders. It disperses it and
thereby *[par là]* preserves it, preserves her, in an
instant.

— He (but perhaps it is she, *la* cinder) perhaps he
knows what he thus wished to set on fire, to celebrate,
to ignite with praise in the secret of the sentence,

perhaps they still know it, perhaps he knows at least something about it. But even tonight he may still discover what is unknown or unconscious in this saying that he sometimes says he has read and sometimes, I recall his expression, forged. He had pronounced it with an English accent, my "counterfeiter's forgery." He will of course die someday; and for however brief a time, the little phrase has some chance of surviving him, more a cinder than ever, there, and less than ever without anyone to say "I."

— But the counterfeiter can lie, he's lying, I am almost sure of it, from experience. There is doubtless no real secret at the bottom of this sentence, no determined proper name. Once he confided to me, but I still do not believe that the first letter of almost every word, I.L.Y.A.L.C. *[il y a là cendre]*, was the first letter of another word, all of it expressing, but in a foreign language, an entirely different statement, which would have played the role of a coded proper name, in truth his ciphered signature. I believed none of it, he had just invented the hoax, he can always lie or not even be certain of what he claims to know. It is precisely at this point that the cinder is there. If he were sure of the truth of his knowledge, why would he have this desire to write and above all to publish a phrase that makes itself indeterminate in this way? Why set adrift and "clandestine" in

this way such a readable proposition? His proposition, that there may be cinder there, finally consists, in its extreme fragility and in the little time at its disposal (its life will have been so short), of this nonknowledge toward which writing and recognition, always a pair, are precipitated. One and the other, both of them, are compelled into the same crypt.

— Through the patient, tormenting, ironic return of the exegesis that leads to nothing and which the unsophisticated would find unseemly, would we be molding the urn of a language for this cinder sentence, which he, he, has abandoned to its chance and to fate, a self-destructive virtue firing on its own right into the heart?

— But the urn of language is so fragile. It crumbles and immediately you blow into the dust of words that are the cinder itself. And if you entrust it to paper, it is all the better to inflame you with, my dear; you will eat yourself up immediately. No, this is not the tomb he would have dreamed of in order that there may be a place, there may be good reason [y ait lieu], as they say, for the work of mourning to take its time. In this sentence I see the tomb of a tomb, the monument of an impossible tomb—forbidden, like the memory of a cenotaph, deprived of the patience of mourning,

denied also the slow decomposition that shelters, locates, lodges, hospitalizes itself in you while you eat the pieces (he did not want to eat the piece but was forced to). An incineration celebrates perhaps the nothing of the all, its destruction without return but mad with its desire and with its cunning (all the better to preserve everything, my dear), the desperately disseminal affirmation but also just the opposite, the categorical "no" to the laborious work of mourning, a "no" of fire. How to accept working for His Highness Mourning?

— How can one not accept it? That is what mourning is, the history of its refusal, the narrative of your revolution, your rebellion, my angel, when it enters into history and at midnight you marry a prince. As for the urn of the spoken tongue, even were [fût] it a tongue of fire, do not think that it breaks up easily. And do not lie, you well know how solid a sentence is. By its very disappearance it resists so very many eclipses, it always has a chance of returning; it "incenses" itself to infinity. This is so much more certain finally than placing the archive in a reinforced beam destined for our extraterrestrial cousins. The sentence is adorned with all of its dead. And all the better to eat yourself with, say the grandmother and the wolf for whom you work; it is still to the benefit of mourning.

37

III

"... And to finish that Second Letter: '... Consider these facts and take care lest you sometime come to repent of having now unwisely published your views. It is a very great safeguard to learn by heart instead of writing ... to me graphein all'ekmanthanien. ... It is impossible for what is written not to be disclosed. That is the reason why I have never written anything about these things ... oud'estin sungramma Platonos ouden oud'estai, and why there is not and will not be any written work of Plato's own. What are now called his ... Sokratous estin kalou kai neou gegonotos ... are the work of a Socrates embellished and modernized. Farewell and believe. Read this letter now at once many times and burn it. ...'

—I hope this one won't get lost. Quick, a duplicate ... graphite ... carbon ... reread this letter ... burn it. There are cinders there, cinders there are [Il y a là cendre]. And now, to distinguish, between two repetitions ...

38

— If it were I, I would have preferred never to have written that, I would have burnt it at once.

— Was *[fut]* that not done?

— You just said that he could not have an "up to date" phrase for this cinder word. Yes, there is perhaps only one worth publishing; it would tell of the all-burning, otherwise called holocaust and the crematory oven, in German in all the Jewish languages of the world.

— You say you no longer remember the place where the legend, a second time, in the same book, like Plato murmuring in the enclosure of the pharmacy . . .

— A perfumed murmur, the pharmakon sometimes designates a kind of incense, and the second iteration, which looks like a citation, which pretends to be a citation, but it only starts up all over again the first time and the last time at the same time. If you no longer recall it, it is because the incineration follows its course and the consummation proceeds from itself, the cinder itself. Trace destined, like everything, to disappear from itself, as much in order to lose the way as to rekindle a memory. The cinder is exact: because without a trace it precisely traces more than an other, and as the other trace(s). Although it comes earlier in

39

The night passes. In the morning, knocks are heard at the door.

They seem to be coming from outside, this time . . .

Two knocks . . . four . . ."

IV

"I hope this one won't get lost. Quick, a duplicate . . . graphite . . . carbon . . . reread this letter . . . burn it. And now, to distinguish two repetitions . . .

The night passes. In the morning, knocks are heard at the door.

They seem to be coming from outside, this time . . .

Three knocks . . ."

V

"27 August 1979. You just called. Ah no, above all not Phoenix (which for me, moreover, is first of all, in my fundamental language, the mark . . ."

the book, on an earlier page, it was *[fut]* inscribed there after its second iteration on the book's last page: it did not figure in the first version of the text. Between the two versions, where is the cinder of the other, here or there?

— Now, through this precise return of the cinders, and for a long time I have observed you when you write, what returns from the breathless race makes its way on a long cinder track. No matter how much you resist it, you have mass and volume only when covered with cinders, as one covers one's head with ashes in a sign of mourning.

— There is rebellion against the Phoenix and also the affirmation of the fire without place or mourning.

— The sentence remains visible for me and even before rereading it, its image in my memory is imprinted in the plural: there are cinders there, cinders there are. A faulty version to be buried, as do the Jews when a manuscript has wounded the name of God. The "s," silent so that it cannot be heard and to change nothing in the hearing, my memory played with that; and with the singular homophone *[cendre]* it played a game more discriminating, more reassuring, no doubt. But this "there" from now on signified that the innumerable lurks beneath the cinder. Incubation of the fire lurking beneath the dust.

41

VI

"As for the 'Envois' themselves, I do not know if reading them is bearable. You might consider them, if you really wish to, as the remainders of a recently destroyed correspondence. Destroyed by fire or by that which figuratively takes its place, more certain of leaving nothing out of the reach of what I like to call the tongue of fire, not even the cinders if there are cinders there [s'il y a là cendre]. *Save* [fors] *a chance."*

VII

"For the totally incinerated envois *could not be indicated by any mark."*

VIII

"If you had listened to me, you would have burned everything, and nothing would have arrived. I mean on the contrary that something ineffaceable would have arrived, in the place of . . ."

IX

"Nothing has arrived because you wanted to preserve (and therefore to lose), which in effect formed the sense of the

— The fire: what one cannot extinguish in this trace among others that is a cinder. Memory or oblivion, as you wish, but of the fire, trait that still relates to the burning. No doubt the fire has withdrawn, the conflagration has been subdued, but if cinder there is, it is because the fire remains in retreat. By its retreat it still feigns having abandoned the terrain. It still camouflages, it disguises itself, beneath the multiplicity, the dust, the makeup powder, the insistent pharmakon of a plural body that no longer belongs to itself—not to remain nearby itself, not to belong to itself, there is the essence of the cinder, its cinder itself.

— Above the sacred place, incense again, but no monument, no Phoenix, no erection that stands—or falls, the cinder without ascension, the cinders love me, they change sex, they re-cinder themselves, they androgynocide themselves.

— She plays with words as one plays with fire, I would denounce her as a pyromaniac who wants to make us forget that in Sicily churches are built with the stone of lava. Pyrotechnical writing feigns abandoning everything to what goes up in smoke, leaving there only cinder that does not remain. I would set out a long narrative, of names, Mallarmé, the history of tobacco, Baudelaire's "Counterfeit Money," Mauss's *The Gift*, "The whole soul summed up

43

order coming from behind my voice, you remember, so many years ago, in my first 'true' letter: 'burn everything.'"

X

"... then you added) 'I am burning. I have the stupid impression of being faithful to you. I am nonetheless saving certain simulacra from your sentences [you have shown them to me since]. I am waking up. I remember the cinders. What a chance, to burn, yes, yes . . .'"

XI

"The symbol! A great holocaustic fire, a burn-everything into which we would throw finally, along with our entire memory, our names, the letters, photos, small objects, keys, fetishes, etc."

XII

"Holocaust of the children

God himself
had only the choice between two crematory ovens . . ."

XIII

"They will see it only through the fire (they will only be blinded by it)."

XIV

"In the final account, the first chance or the first reckoning, the great burning of this summer. You'll be there, say it, at the last moment, one match each to start. [. . .] We will draw close to the fire on a day of judgment, perhaps,

44

it will be at least the third time that I play with the fire on that day, and each time for the most serious stakes."

XV

"But in principle only, and if fire's share is impossible to delimit, by virtue of the lexicon and the 'themes,' it is not for the usual reason (give fire its due, light counterfires in order to stop the progression of a blaze, avoid a holocaust). On the contrary, the necessity of the whole [du tout] announces itself . . ."

XVI

" . . . I will never get there, the contamination is everywhere and we would never light the fire. Language poisons for us the most secret of our secrets. One can no longer even burn at home, in peace, trace the circle of a hearth; one must even sacrifice one's own sacrifice to it."

XVII

"and when you will no longer come back, after the fire, I will still send you virgin and mute cards; you will no longer recognize even the memories of our travels and our common places, but you will know that I am faithful to you."

XVIII

"Doubtless this was the first desired holocaust (as one says a desired child, a desired girl)."

XIX

"There [Là] especially where I speak truly they will be blinded by the fire. On this subject, you know that Freud's Sophie was cremated. He, too."

XX

"Tomorrow I will write you again, in our foreign language. I won't remember a word of it and in September, without my having even seen it again, you will burn,

you will burn it,

it has to be you."

[. . .] however slightly The cinder separates itself [. . .] The overly precise meaning erases Your vague literature."

— With these citations, these references, you authorize the cinder, you will construct a new university, perhaps. But listen to Virginia Woolf in *Three Guineas*: "No guinea of earned money [money earned by the women] should go to rebuilding the college on the old plan; just as certainly none could be spent upon building a college upon a new plan; therefore the guinea should be earmarked 'Rags. Petrol. Matches.' And this note should be attached to it: 'Take this guinea and with it burn the college to the ground. Set fire to the old hypocrisies. Let the light of the burning building scare the nightingales and incarnadine the willows. And let the daughters of educated men dance round the fire and heap armful upon armful of dead leaves upon the flames. And let their mothers lean from the upper windows and cry, Let it blaze! Let it blaze! For we have done with this "education"!'"

— One must still know how to "let it blaze." One must be good at it. There is also Nietzsche's paradox—which makes him something else perhaps than a thinker of the totality of entities *[l'étant]*—when he no longer normalizes the relation of the cinder to the whole by treating it as part of the whole, or by

49

introducing some tranquilizing metonymic logos: "Our entire world is the *cinder* of innumerable *living* beings; and what is living is so little in relation to the whole, it must be that, once already, *everything* was transformed into life and it will continue to be so." Or elsewhere *(Gay Science)*: "Let us guard against saying that death is opposed to life. The living being is only a species of what is dead, and a very rare species."

— In the first legend, which comes after the second, after her, the movement of the dedication (recognition of debt and nonrestitution) says at least, shows by barely saying that the cinder comes in place of the gift. Gift there would have been, even if it is not said, as it should be so that it may take place, from whatever or whomever. Recognition and denial of a debt, of a "single divided trait," "far from the center." And from a mere letter, from a *d/t* thrown through the teeth ("Though the letter gains strength solely from this indirection"), a center crumbles and dissolves, it is dispersed in a throw of the die: cinder.

— Mute, the dedication feigns restitution. But it knows only how to render or give nothing but fiery dust; it says nothing, it allows nothing of itself to appear, of its origin or its destination, only a trail in the sand, and it still anesthetizes you: can you not feel the step *[pas]* into the burning sand? In the

place of others, plural already, of their names and not of themselves, there are cinders there, "of the others, cinders there are."

— It is obviously a figure, although no face lets itself be seen. The name "cinder" figures, and because there is no cinder here, not here (nothing to touch, no color, no body, only words), but above all because these words, which through the name are supposed to name not the word but the thing, they are what names one thing in the place of another, metonymy when the cinder is separated, one thing while figuring another from which nothing figurable remains.

— A word, unfit even to name the cinder in the place of the memory of something else, and no longer referring back to it, how can a word ever present itself? The word, like the cinder, similar to her, comparable to the point of hallucination. Cinder, the word, is never found here, but there.

— For that it is necessary that you take the word into your mouth, when you breathe, whence the cinder comes to the vocable, which disappears from sight, like burning semen, like lava destined nowhere. Cinder is only a word. But what is a word for consuming itself all the way to its support (the tape-recorded voice or strip of paper, self-destruction

53

of the impossible emission once the order is given), to the point of assimilating it without apparent remainder? And you can also receive semen through the ear.

— What a difference between cinder and smoke: the latter apparently gets lost, and better still, without perceptible remainder, for it rises, it takes to the air, it is spirited away, sublimated. The cinder—falls, tires, lets go, more material since it fritters away its word; it is very divisible.

— I understand that the cinder is nothing that can be in the world, nothing that remains as an entity *[étant]*. It is the being *[l'être]*, rather, that there is—this is a name of the being that there is there but which, giving itself *(es gibt ashes)*, is nothing, remains beyond everything that is *(konis epekeina tes ousias)*, remains unpronounceable in order to make saying it possible although it is nothing.

— My desire only goes so far as the invisible distance, immediately "grilled" between languages, overrunning the distance between *cendre, cenere,* ashes, cinders, *cinis, Asche, cendrier* (a whole sentence), *Aschenbecher,* ashtray, etc., and *cineres,* and above all the *ceniza* of Francisco de Quevedo, his sonnets "To Vesuvius */Al Vesubio,*" and "I am cinder that darkens in the flame / nothing that remains to consume

XXI

"Before my death I would give orders. If you aren't there, my body is to be pulled out of the lake [lac] *and burned, my ashes are to be sent to you, the urn well protected ('fragile') but not registered, in order to tempt fate. This would be an* envoi *of/from me* [un envoi de moi] *that no longer would come from me (or an* envoi *sent by me, who would have ordered it, but no longer an* envoi *of me, as you like). And then you would enjoy mixing my cinders with what you*

56

the fire / that in amorous conflagration" [is dispersed], and "will be cinder, but will remain sentient / will be dust, but amorous dust" / "*Yo soy ceniza que sobró a la llama; / nada, dejó por consumir el fuego, / que en amoroso incendio se derrama [. . .] serán ceniza, mas tendrán sentido; / polvo serán, mas polvo enamorado.*"

— I hear well, I hear it, for I still have an ear for the flame even if a cinder is silent, as if he burned paper at a distance, with a lens, a concentration of light as a result of seeing in order not to see, writing in the passion of nonknowledge rather than of the secret. I would say, for the protection and illustration of its own sentence; "I" the cinder would say that his writing is not interested in knowledge. The raw cinder, that is more to his taste; and the initial consonant matters very little. Every word seems to finish with *–endre,* or *–andre,* verb, proper or common noun, and even a verb that becomes an attribute: *le tendre.* What does he do with –DRE, I ask myself: *sans-, sens-, sang-, cent-* DRE. I leave it to you to find examples.

— And with this lack that is *la* cendre, these *lac*(k)*s,* this *lac*(k)(s)—when he gets all entangled with telepathy, there *[là]* also *LA* Cinder is there.

— No, you treat his phrase like the accumulation

eat (morning coffee, brioche, tea at 5 o'clock, etc.). After a certain dose, you would start to go numb, to fall in love with yourself; I would watch you slowly advance toward death, you would approach me within you with a serenity that we have no idea of, absolute reconciliation. And you would give orders . . . While waiting for you I'm going to sleep, you're always there, my sweet love."

of surplus value, as if he speculated on some cinder capital. It is, however, a question of making a withdrawal, in order to let him try his luck on a gift without the least memory of itself, in the final account, through a corpus, a pile of cinders unconcerned about preserving its form, a retreat, a retracing only without any relation with what, now, through love, I just did and I am just about to tell you—

SOURCES FOR ANIMADVERSIONS

   I *Dissemination,* trans. Barbara Johnson (Chicago: University of Chicago Press, 1981), 366.

  II *Glas,* trans. John P. Leavey Jr. and Richard Rand (Lincoln: University of Nebraska Press, 1986), 238–43.

  III "Plato's Pharmacy," in *Dissemination,* 170–71.

  IV "La Pharmacie de Platon," *Tel Quel* 33 (1968): 59.

  V *The Postcard,* trans. Alan Bass (Chicago: University of Chicago Press, 1987), 254.

  VI *The Postcard,* 3.

  VII *The Postcard,* 5.

  VIII *The Postcard,* 23.

  IX *The Postcard,* 23.

  X *The Postcard,* 23.

  XI *The Postcard,* 40.

  XII *The Postcard,* 143.

  XIII *The Postcard,* 182.

  XIV *The Postcard,* 198.

  XV *The Postcard,* 222.

  XVI *The Postcard,* 224.

  XVII *The Postcard,* 245.

  XVIII *The Postcard,* 254.

  XIX *The Postcard,* 255.

  XX *The Postcard,* 256.

  XXI *The Postcard,* 196.

Translations have been modified from the published English translations for Animadversions I, II, III, VI, X, XIV, XV, XIX, XX, and XXI.

TRANSLATOR'S NOTES

These notes are keyed to page numbers in this book.

3 *Feu la cendre* was published as a book and as a recorded cassette tape with Jacques Derrida and Carole Bouquet reading aloud the published text. Just as we have rendered *Feu la cendre* (literally, *Fire, Ash*) as *Cinders*, we will at times throughout the translation render the refrain *il y a la cendre* as "cinders there are," and the refrain *il y a là cendre* (with the accent grave that turns the definite article into an adverb) as "there are cinders there" in order to express not only that cinders are someplace, that they exist in some fashion, but that they also exist "there," in a particular place and time, which enables the silent play of *la/là*, with or without the accent grave, to be read and thus enables the enigmatic oscillation between an existential "thereness" and a situated "thereness" to become readable even when it remains inaudible. This interplay of voice and writing, and the impossibility of maintaining it, motivates the entire project of *Feu la cendre*, which is why the translation will render the inaudible accent grave on *là cendre* as both "there are cinders there" and "cinders there are."

19 *Fors la cendre*, "nothing but the cinder," but also *for la cendre*, as in *le for intérieur*, one's innermost sense, thus "the innermost cinder." *Le four*, the furnace or oven, is not far off.

19–21 *Un lieu pur se chiffrât-il.* Derrida echoes the "taking

63

place" of "place" ("rien n'aura eu lieu que le lieu") *dans ces parages du vague*, "in these vague regions," from Stéphane Mallarmé's "Un Coup de dés," where it is a question of hallucination, agony, and the unconcealment of the concealment of the origin of number ("le nombre". . . *clos quand apparu*), where it is a question of "tallying up the whole" ("se chiffrât-il"/*évidence de la somme*).

19 *Pur est le mot. Pur = Pyr,* Greek for "fire." Thus, *pyrification.*

21 *Tombe en tant que nom. Tombe,* as a noun, is "tomb"; as a verb, it means "falls."

23 *Encenser,* to praise or extol as well as to burn incense, also sounds like *insensé,* insane or maddened; the English *incense* or *incensed* contains all these meanings.

33 "Clandestining" is the inevitable effect that the cinder *envoi* has on the sending of any letter.

37 *Rien du tout,* "nothing at all" or "the nothing of the all."

39 Although the saying *il y a là cendre* appears in "Plato's Pharmacy" prior to its appearance in the dedicatory *envoi* at the very end of *Dissemination,* this allusion was in fact written after the one in the concluding acknowledgments. In distinguishing between the repetitions at work here, Derrida is reminded of Plato "mutter[ing] . . . [i]n the enclosed space of the pharmacy" as he begins to analyze the *pharmakon* (*Dissemination* 169). In "Plato's Pharmacy" and more recently in "Chôra" [in *Poikilia: Études Offertes à Jean-Pierre Vernant* (Paris: Éditions de L'École des hautes études en sciences sociales, 1987), 265–96], Derrida presents *chôra* as Plato's most challenging version of this "enclosed space," the "place" rather, the "mother and receptacle of this generated world" (*Timaeus* 51a), "there" between the unchanging Forms *(eidos)* on the outside and the mutable copies *(eikon)* on the inside.

41 "Cinders" in English makes the silent "s" in "cendres" audible. Here we might cite from T. E. Hulme's "Cinders," the final section of his *Speculations* (1924): "That the world is finite [. . .] and that it is yet an infinitude of cinders." Emmanuel Levinas has written of the Jewish custom of burying a faulty manuscript.

49 Derrida's caesura is formed from four of the fourteen lines of Mallarmé's sonnet "Toute l'âme résumée" in *Hommages et Tombeaux*, where Mallarmé compares the expiration of the soul to the separation of the ash from the burning cinder *(la cendre se sépare / De son clair baiser de feu)* in a well-smoked cigar *(quelque cigare / Brûlant savamment)*. Here lies perhaps a trace of the promised "history of tobacco." Incidentally, Baudelaire's prose poem "Counterfeit Money" concerns a "singularly minute repartitioning" of the notion of the gift that occurs as two friends exit a tobacconist's shop. Derrida analyzes Mauss and Baudelaire in detail in *Donner le temps (Given Time)* (Paris: Galilée, 1991).

51 The first Nietzsche citation is from notes made in 1881 during the composition of *The Gay Science* (Friedrich Nietzsche, *Idyllen aus Messina / Die fröhliche Wissenschaft / Nachgelassene Fragmente Frühjahr 1881 bis Sommer 1882*, in *Kritische Gesamtausgabe: Werke*, pt. 5, vol. 2, eds. Giorgio Colli and Mazzino Montinari [Berlin: Walter de Gruyter, 1973], 370–71).

51 The mortal throw of the die that is the exhalation of a vocable at once delivers the gift and the debt, dissemination and grace, the necessity and impossibility of return. Thus cinders fall to ash: *dé:cendre.*

51 *Sable brûlant ou pas,* "burning sand or not," also suggests the heat of the nonnegative "step," the *pas*, the "stop" or

65

obstruction to which we can be so anesthetized that we no longer feel the nonpresence burning within language.

53 The "impossible emission" recalls, of course, the TV series *Mission: Impossible.*

55 *Konis epekeina tes ousias* (cinders beyond being or presence) rewrites Plato's *agathon epekeina tes ousias* (the good beyond being).

57 *Griller une distance* means "to overrun a distance," here in the sense of being unable to stop because the very notion of a distance between languages has been annulled. The burning and the grilling begin as soon as one steps beyond a language and toward language itself.

57 "For the defense and illustration of the French language" is an expression of L'Académie Française.

59 *Tendre,* like the English "tender" or "to tender," means something delicate or fragile that is extended or tendered within language; it rhymes with *cendre.* The four words considered in relation to –DRE translate to "without," "sense," "blood," and "hundred."

59 The phrase *pas un corpus,* "not a corpus," appears in the 1982 text of *Feu la cendre.* The 1987 version changes/corrects this phrase to *par un corpus,* "by [or through] a corpus."

posthumanities

CARY WOLFE, SERIES EDITOR

Jacques Derrida (1930–2004) was a French philosopher associated with the poststructuralist and postmodernist movements. He is best known for developing the concept of deconstruction. He published more than forty books, including *Of Grammatology, Writing and Difference,* and *Speech and Phenomena.*

Ned Lukacher is professor emeritus of English at the University of Illinois at Chicago.

Cary Wolfe is Bruce and Elizabeth Dunlevie Professor of English at Rice University.